JOSEPH MIDTHUN   SAMUEL HITI

BUILDING BLOCKS OF SCIENCE

LIGHT

WORLD
BOOK

a Scott Fetzer company
Chicago
www.worldbook.com

World Book, Inc.
233 N. Michigan Avenue
Chicago, IL 60601
U.S.A.

For information about other World Book publications, visit our website at http://www.worldbook.com or call 1-800-WORLDBK (967-5325).

For information about sales to schools and libraries, call 1-800-975-3250 (United States); 1-800-837-5365 (Canada).

Library of Congress Cataloging-in-Publication Data

Light.
    p. cm. -- (Building blocks of science)
    Includes index.
    Summary: "A graphic nonfiction volume that introduces the properties of light. Features include several photographic pages, a glossary, additional resource list, and an index"--Provided by publisher.
    ISBN 978-0-7166-1426-5
    1. Light--Juvenile literature. I. World Book, Inc.
QC360.L536 2012
535--dc23
                    2011025977

Building Blocks of Science
Set ISBN: 978-0-7166-1420-3 (print, hc.)

Also available as ISBN:
978-0-7166-1468-5 (pbk.)

E-book editions:
ISBN 978-0-7166-1865-2 (EPUB3)
ISBN 978-0-7166-1444-9 (PDF)

Acknowledgments:
Created by Samuel Hiti and Joseph Midthun.
Art by Samuel Hiti. Written by Joseph Midthun.

© Adam Burton, Alamy Images 6; © Brian Harris, Alamy Images 16; © FORGET Patrick/SAGAPHOTO/ Alamy Images 13; © Mark Sunderland, Alamy Images 13; © Peter Alvey, Alamy Images 12; © RIA Novosti/ Alamy Images 7; © Igor Plotnikov, Shutterstock 17

Printed in China by Leo Paper Products, LTD., Heshan Guangdong
3rd printing June 2014

ATTENTION, READER!

Some characters in this series throw large objects from tall buildings, play with fire, ride on bicycle handlebars, and perform other dangerous acts. However, they are CARTOON CHARACTERS. Please do not try any of these things at home because you could seriously harm yourself—or others around you!

STAFF
Executive Committee
President: Donald D. Keller
Vice President and Editor in Chief: Paul A. Kobas.
Vice President, Sales & Marketing:
    Sean Lockwood
Vice President, International: Richard Flower
Director, Human Resources: Bev Ecker

Editorial
Manager, Supplementary Publications:
    Cassie Mayer
Writer and Letterer: Joseph Midthun
Editors: Mike DuRoss and Brian Johnson
Researcher: Annie Brodsky
Manager, Contracts & Compliance
    (Rights & Permissions): Loranne K. Shields

Manufacturing/Pre-Press/Graphics and Design
Director: Carma Fazio
Manufacturing Manager: Steven Hueppchen
Production/Technology Manager:
    Anne Fritzinger
Proofreader: Emilie Schrage
Senior Manager, Graphics and Design: Tom Evans
Coordinator, Design Development and
    Production: Brenda B. Tropinski
Book Design: Samuel Hiti
Photographs Editor: Kathy Creech

TABLE OF CONTENTS

There is a glossary on page 30. Terms defined in the glossary are in type **that looks like this** on their first appearance.

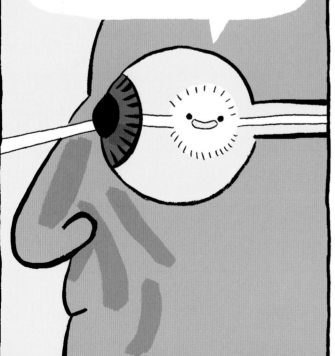

Natural light comes from the sun.

It looks white to you.

This is the light that allows you to see.

Without light, you would not have food to eat or air to breathe.

That's because plants and many kinds of ocean life use light from the sun to make food and oxygen.

All the food you eat and the oxygen you breathe can be traced to these living things, and therefore to me!

The energy in fuels also comes from sunlight.

Fossil fuels are made from the remains of living things that died millions of years ago.

All the energy in these fuels originally came from sunlight.

People use these fuels to produce electric power and to operate machines.

MOVING LIGHT ALONG...

Light can pass through some materials easily and others not at all.

Opaque objects don't let light pass through. They absorb some light and reflect the rest.

This brick wall is opaque. You can't see through it.

Shadows form when an opaque object blocks the path of light.

Transparent objects let most of the light pass through. You can see through them!

This glass window is transparent.

What about a stained-glass window?

It's a **translucent** object.

It lets some light pass through, but only certain colors.

It can also **scatter** the light, making objects on the other side look blurry.

WHAT ARE COLORS?

White light is made of all the colors of a rainbow.

Red, orange, yellow, green, blue, indigo, and violet...

...ROY G BIV for short!

Each color has a different wavelength.

Light with longer wavelengths is red.

Light with shorter wavelengths is violet.

The other colors have wavelengths between red and violet.

Together, they make up all the colors of a rainbow.

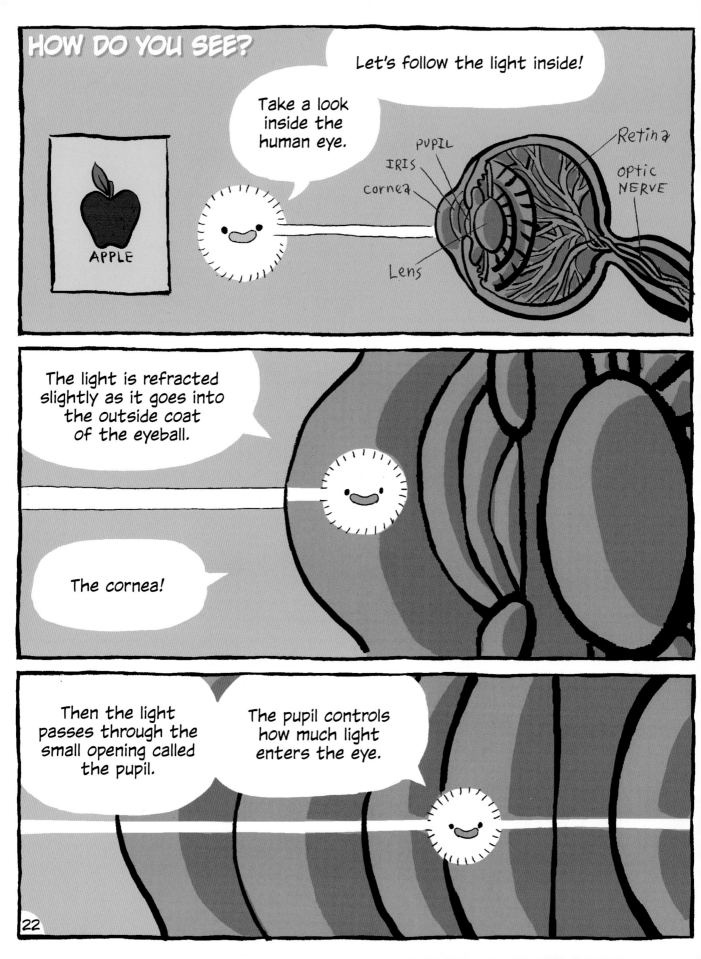

The light then travels through the lens.

The lens refracts the light so that it strikes the retina as a clear image.

The image that the lens focuses onto the retina is upside down.

APPLE

The retina changes the image into signals that your brain can understand.

The brain then uses the signal to make a picture. It also flips the image around.

APPLE

The visible light spectrum includes all the colors of the rainbow.

But there are many other forms of light that you can't see!

INFRARED WAVES

Here are a few examples of this "invisible" light.

ULTRAVIOLET WAVES

RADIO WAVES

X-RAYS

Bees and other insects use ultraviolet light to see where a flower has nectar!

All of the different kinds of light make up the **electromagnetic spectrum.**

ELECTROMAGNETIC SPECTRUM

Right now, scientists are searching the skies with telescopes that can see light that you can't.

One of these instruments, the Hubble Space Telescope, is orbiting in space around Earth.

It has produced detailed images captured from the far reaches of the universe.

But how humans use light in the future is up to you!

See you around!

29

GLOSSARY

absorb to take in and hold rather than reflect.

concave lens a lens that is thicker at the edges than in the center. Objects appear smaller when viewed through a concave lens.

convex lens a lens that is thicker in the center than at the edges. Objects appear larger when viewed through a convex lens.

distance the amount of space between two points.

electromagnetic spectrum the entire range of electromagnetic energy, including visible light and forms of light that cannot be seen by the human eye. Electromagnetic energy is made up of electric and magnetic waves.

opaque describes an object that does not allow light to pass through it.

prism a special piece of glass or plastic that can refract (bend) light to produce a spectrum of colors.

reflect to throw back light, heat, sound, or other form of energy. Reflection occurs when energy or an object bounces off a surface.

refract what occurs when light bends as it passes from one substance to another.

scatter to separate and drive off in different directions.

speed the distance traveled in a certain time.

translucent describes an object that allows only some light to pass through it.

transparent describes an object that allows nearly all light to pass through it.

visible spectrum the band of colors that make up white light.

wavelength the distance between peaks of a wave.

FIND OUT MORE

Books

I See Myself by Vicki Cobb and Julia Gorton (HarperCollins Publishers, 2002)

Light and Optics by John Farndon (Benchmark Books, 2001)

All About Light by Lisa Trumbauer (Children's Press, 2004)

Dazzling Science Projects with Light and Color by Robert Gardner and Tom LaBaff (Enslow Elementary, 2006)

Light: Shadows, Mirrors, and Rainbows by Natalie M. Rosinsky and Sheree Boyd (Picture Window Books, 2003)

The Science of Light and Color by Patricia Miller-Schroeder (Gareth Stevens Publishing, 2000)

Color by John Farndon (Benchmark Books, 2001)

Day Light, Night Light: Where Light Comes From by Franklyn Mansfield Branley and Stacey Schuett (HarperCollins Publishers, 1998)

Websites

Colors of Light
http://www.mhschool.com/science/2000/student/5/review/summary/5-3-6-6.html
This educational site from McGraw-Hill Science includes a multiple-choice quiz to test your knowledge of light and color.

Exploratorium: Science Snacks About Light
http://www.exploratorium.edu/snacks/iconlight.html
Simple experiments let you play with light and its effects at this educational website.

Human Body Videos: The Eye
http://www.sciencekids.co.nz/videos/humanbody/eye.html
At this site from Science Kids, watch how the different parts of the eye work together in an educational video. Then check out fun facts about the eye!

Light for Kids
http://www.sciencekids.co.nz/light.html
Cool games, videos, and lessons take you into the worlds of light and color at this Science Kids page.

Make a Splash with Color!
http://www.thetech.org/exhibits/online/color/intro/
Learn how your eyes help you see the world in all its many colors at this educational website from the Tech Museum.

Optics for Kids: Exploring the Science of Light
http://www.optics4kids.org/
Explore optical illusions, important terms, and the lives of scientists who are using optics for important discoveries and inventions.

The Science of Light
http://www.learner.org/teacherslab/science/light/
Here, you can learn about the laws of light and color through online activities that let you mix colors and play around with fun house mirrors.

INDEX